TEACHER

of

JESSO PLAQUES

MOLDS

FIGURINE MAKING

by D. M. CAMPANA

Campana's Popular Art Library

D. M. CAMPANA ART CO.

CHICAGO : : ILLINOIS

INDEX

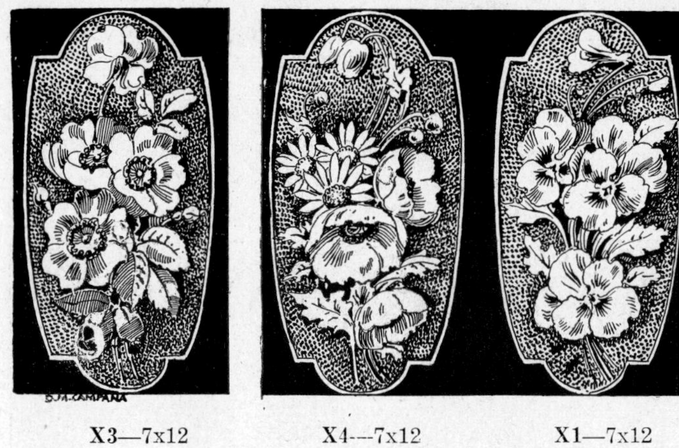

X3—7x12   X4—7x12   X1—7x12

HOW TO PAINT PLAQUES

is explained on these pages. From these suggestions you can paint any other plaque.

In order to help some worker that is not acquainted with the painting of plaques we will give an idea of various colors used in various shades, and though there is no rule in art and what is suggested to you may be changed to what you like with the same good result, we think that some of our readers may like to know a little about color combinations.

We suggest that you use oil colors because they are more brilliant and more easily handled. You can easily mix them, make them light and make them dark, simply by adding one or two colors, and they always make a good clean surface to your decoration over Relief.

There are persons who use Japan colors because they dry quicker, but to us they are not as pretty as the oil. There are other people using lacquers, but to our taste the lacquers are a little too gaudy. Furthermore they fade. However, after you have tried this and that you may use your own judgment and learn by enjoying your experimenting.

When your oil colors are dry, which generally takes twenty-four hours or over, you apply a coating of varnish as that will keep the colors from getting muddy or dusty.

In some other paragraph we have explained how to apply Pearline to make the effect different and so forth, but our main suggestion is that you should not feel afraid or awkward in

[4]

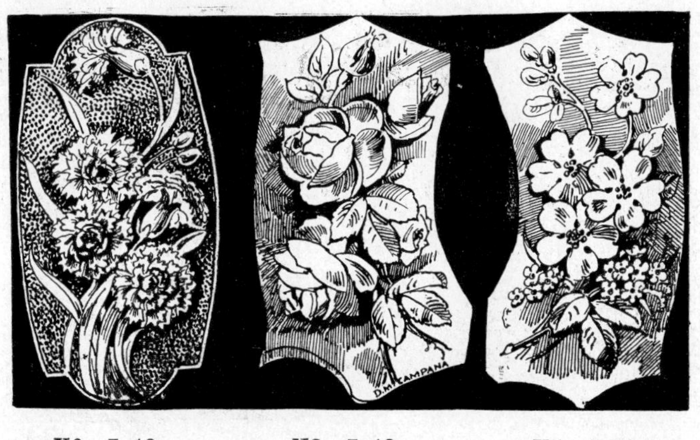

X6—7x12   X2—7x12   X5—7x12

trying to use your own judgment in colors and everything and if you do not like it when it is dry you can go over it again and change the color effect entirely.

A good color for the plaque X-3, wild roses, is vermillion mixed with white, and you use as much white as necessary to make a delicate tint. One or two of the wild roses can be made by using a little carmine mixed with the white, which would give you an entirely different tint and make a good combination with the first shade. The center is in orange-yellow and the background is preferable in the dark, so as to carry out the delicate tint of the roses. For the green you can use either Chrome green, light and dark, or emerald green, always made light by the addition of a lighter color, either a light yellow or white. That will give a kind of a pastel effect to the plaque. As we say, a darker background would be in Payne's gray or cobalt blue and a trifle of black. The edge around the plaque would be made in gold bronze or it can be kept of the same color as the background of the plaque itself. Small details in the flowers or in the leaves can be applied toward the end, and when everything is applied you should let it dry before a coat of varnish is applied all over the background, roses and everything.

Plaque X-2 is very well carried out and makes a decorative article by using carmine mixed with white and for the center of the rose use the same carmine only with less white. You could make one rose in the pink as given and the other one in the dark tone, like with the carmine pure, making a good combination.

[5]

X7—7x12   X8—7x12   X15—7x12

The background of this plaque would be in a light gray, as for instance a Payne's gray and white. The green leaves you can make with the various greens which you have.

X-1. The pansies allow a large variety of colors, such as Vandyke brown, orange, vermillion, lemon yellow, mauve and almost any color, because you can find the pansy in almost any color that you have on your palette. Naturally, you make them all different colors and in this case we would suggest a darker background, such as Vandyke brown or even black.

X-5. The apple blossom can be carried out in very light colors as for instance the flowers in white with a touch of vermillion so as to have them nearly white, and the forget-me-not with a cobalt and a good deal of white to make a delicate shade. For the leaves we would suggest dark chrome green with white and the center of the flowers are in a little touch of pink tone.

We suggest the background in a very delicate tone by using mauve or purple and a good deal of white, as this warm color would make a good combination with the delicate color of the flowers.

X-4. The poppies and daisies plaque is easily understood to be red poppies and white daisies on a dark background, but it can be changed by making yellow daisies and white poppies, or one poppy white and one or two in red.

It is interesting for the worker to try things especially because if you make a mistake and a color doesn't look good you can apply another color over it with a very satisfactory result. The vermillion would be the best color for the red poppy, and

[6]

X14
American Beauties 9x10½

X10—7x12   X11—7x12

if you wish to make California poppies you could use the
orange. Make the background dark, either a dark brown or
black. and as for the edges of all those plaques it is up to
the worker to make them in gold or have a solid color of some
kind, say Lemon yellow.

X-8.   The morning glory plaque is generally in a delicate
blue or violet tint, which can be made by mixing a little
carmine, a little cobalt blue and a good deal of white. The
middle flower can be darker than the lower and the top one
so as to make the combination pretty.

The fence is in light brown and white and the landscape
ought to be in a greenish tint made with white and any kind
of green that you have.

The little house and tree can be made a little heavier color
than the other part.

X-7.   The water lillies can be painted with a solid background of green, suggesting the water, and you may use a
chrome green dark mixed with a good deal of white.

The winding lines can be made with a light yellow color
considerably lighter than the water and the large leaves can
be made with the dark chrome green, much darker than the
water itself.

X-6.   The carnation can be painted in almost any color, as
you know that there are many different kinds of carnations.
Some are in pink, some are in dark red, some are in yellow,
some are white, etc., and by using the dark background, either

[7]

40c Each   13X—7½ x 9   12X—7½ x 9   No. 2X08. 6 in. high
                                                        30c.

brown or black, you will have the opportunity to carry out the flowers to a very good combination of color.

A landscape can be painted by applying at first the sky in Cobalt blue with a little white. We don't know the landscape you intend to paint, but in general, trees are painted in Chrome green, either light or dark. Tree barks in Vandyck brown and a trifle of white. Rocks in Paynes gray and white, water with the same color of the sky plus a trifle of light green and white. Roads in Paynes gray, white and a trifle burnt Sienna. Roofs in burnt Sienna, mountains in blue, white and a trifle Carmine. For figure use flesh color.

As mentioned above we cannot specify exact color as we do not know what kind of landscape you intend to make.

"HOW TO PAINT PLAQUES"

When plaques come out of the mould, they are matt. Matt plaques as they can be painted with Water Colors, and shellaced over when dry. When plaques come to you with a certain gloss, they have been lacquered and can be painted with Oil Colors, or with Japan colors. Their appearance when painted is semi-matt and they can be varnished over when the colors are dry. Egyptian lacquers can also be used over lacquered plaques, and they look very brilliant. They need no further varnish over. But lacquers fade.

Plaques can also be varnished and fine Crystalline poured over while the varnish is wet. By using varied Oil colors for varied spots and before the colors are dry, Chrystalline dusted over the wet colors, make a very catchy effect.

Bronzes, 35c an ounce, are used for the frame, and these bronzes are mixed with bronzing liquid, 15c an ounce, mail 3c. Your plaques can have a Japan black background which dries quick, or a blue, or what not. Students using their wits. often do better work than experts.

[8]

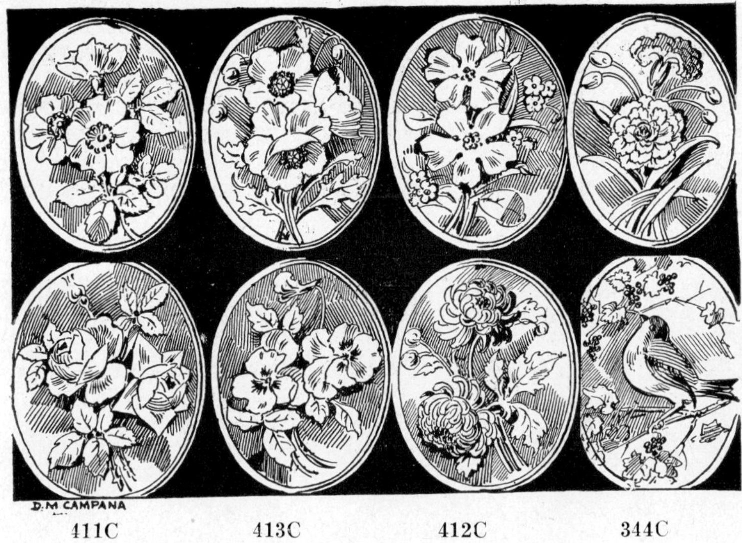

Above Placques are 5¼ x 4¾ — **25c Each**

We always suggest the painting of Plaques with oil colors —(Japan colors dry quickly, oil colors require about 24 hours). However, the oil colors having a shiny appearance and allowing you to paint over and over, are very practical and safe. Mix Carmine with White to paint white roses, to make a sky or blue background, mix Cobalt Blue and White. Greens can be mixed with Light Chrome Yellow and varied shades can be made. Add a little Campana's Pale Drying Oil to make your color soft and well running. As for what color to use, say in a flower plaque, you should not be afraid to experiment. If it does not suit you, you can correct it by going over again. It is always better to apply dark colors first, and light color over, rather than vice versa. We always advise to apply the background at first, make it a fairly dark color or black and your flowers will stand out very nicely. Then paint the flowers and last the leaves. If you use Oil colors, varnish the whole decoration over, provided the colors are dry. If there is a frame around your plaque, cover it up either with color or Gold Bronze. This is a powder, take out some of it in a saucer, add enough of the bronzing medium to make a semi-liquid paste to apply with large brush. Some decorators apply two coatings, but one is often enough. And now your plaque should be complete.

HOW TO START

Presuming that you wish to learn making a plaque. You have at hand one that you want to reproduce. It is best for you to read the directions in this booklet on how to start and proceed.

Read the directions again and again. Naturally you must have the Gypsum, either the Gelatine or the life Rubber, the Grease, etc. and everything mentioned there.

Have all the necessities and all needed instructions; it should not be difficult for you to do the work.

CREATING YOUR OWN DESIGN

A flat plaque is started by building it over a piece of wood or compo board sawed out to the shape and size you want it to be. You can very conveniently use composition clay, called **Plastine** or **Permoplast** or what not. These are clays that remain soft indefinitely and they allow you to model, change and alter your work until it is finished. Other moist clay can be used for modeling but they will dry like a rock. This clay can be kept moist by covering them with a piece of moist rag through the night.

The modeling is better done with modeling sticks or your finger. — Clay will shrink in drying and become smaller. Other composition clays will remain soft and will not shrink. Keep on modeling and detailing until you feel that the work is complete. Then go into the making of the mould.

NEW LIQUID LIFE RUBBER

An elastic solution, invented by Mr. Kiraly, has a big advantage over plaster casting inasmuch as with this material you can cast an unlimited number of reproductions with one single mould. Furthermore, you can utilize the same mould month after month, as it does not deteriorate. With plaster you generally have to break up the mould after you have taken one impression. It has also a big advantage over gelantine casting, because gelantine will eventually spoil and the mould will be useless. It shrinks gradually to small proportions.

The composition used for Kiraly's casting is a secret, but the material can be purchased in either small or large quantities. For instance in cans of one-half pints, pint, one quart, or a gallon. One-half of a pint is sufficient for a small cast, say a piece about 4x5 inches. For a 6x8 inch cast, about three-quarter of a pint is necessary, etc.

DIRECTIONS NO. 1

Take the piece to be reproduced, say a small bust or an ash tray, a small vase, and animal, anything made of metal or earthenware, or wood, glass, plaster, etc. Take a piece of

Ivory Soap or any white soap, take a soft brush, say about one-half inch wide, fill it with water, go over the cake of soap and wash over the article to be casted. Go over again and again, covering every part. Before doing this work, place your flat article on a piece of tinfoil or a very flat metal, or stiff board or a china tray, so that in washing over the article you wash over a certain part of the base surrounding it, say two inches, which part will come in contact with the solution. If your model stands up wash over the place it stands on.

Now open up the can of the LIFE RUBBER LIQUID, fill your brush with the mixture, and began to cover the article all around. Use a well filled brush and do not drag, simply cover every part thickly. Start from the upper part and let it flow down — use plenty of it. Apply the same around the article on the stand, which you have soaped before. Place this coated article in a warm place to set for about thirty minutes, then apply as before another generous coating of the solution. Apply with a full brush, covering every part, also the small space around it on the board, and let it set again as before. Apply now another coating, dry again, etc., until you have applied at least 12 thick coatings. The idea of applying several coatings is to give the solution a chance to dry slowly and properly. When the item is completed, place it in a warm place, but not too hot, and let it stay for at least twenty-four hours or more. In the morning, begin to peel up the solution from the board around the article. Lift up all around, pull it up and begin to get it off the original article, but do it gradually. The cast is so elastic that it will allow you to pull it off and you will have in your hand a soft shell of material, similar to rubber, with a perfect likeness of the original inside. Dust this cast with WHITING or CHALK, then rinse with water. I wish to warn you that if the solution is not very dry, it will be distorted when you pull it off the model. It is now necessary to put a plaster shell around the mold, so that when you cast your reproductions the weight of the plaster may not distort the rubber mold. The illustration gives an idea of the work.   See Page 15 - 16.

If the article has any undercuts, close them up with clay or plastine, or any similar substance. **Undercut** means a deep space or groove that may prevent the plaster from coming loose after it has hardened. Now moisten the cast with soap water, and when dry, cover with any oil, such as OLIVE or RAW LINSEED OIL. This coating is on the reverse side of the molding, where the plaster shell is going to come. Now you place your molding head down on the board, oil up the board one and one-half inches all around. Take some water, say a pint, pour in an open-mouth jar, and add Plaster of Paris little by little until it shows above the water. Now stir very well. Make a mixture as thick as cream. See that there are not lumps or bubbles. Having dipped the mold in water, you now pour this plaster mix over it, going all over covering every part, allowing about fifteen minutes to set, then put on more plaster and flatten it all around. Put on still more, and until you have a shell at least one inch thick. Before it dries, flatten the top, smooth it all around, and let it dry until the plaster is real hard. In thirty to forty minutes the plaster is set, and picking the whole thing up from the board, you will find that the mold inside is in perfect shape and ready for any number of reproductions. If you wish, the mold can be taken out of the shell and put back, and it can be folded and put in your pocket just like a piece of soft rubber. If you wish to purchase any of this LIQUID LIVE RUBBER, write the author of this book, D. M. CAMPANA — Artist — Chicago, Illinois.

NOTICE — Use a soft, good sized brush, say about an inch wide, for the application of the Liquid Rubber over the model. Put in a glass of water when not in use, and on the completion of the whole application, wash well in water.

SPRAYING THE LIQUID RUBBER
DIRECTIONS NO. 2

The **liquid Rubber** can be sprayed on the model instead of applying it with the brush. After you have done the preparation as shown in the beginning of Directions No. 1. You pour in the sprayer glass jar a fair quantity of the liquid Rubber, say about three-quarter full in the glass container so as to allow the small tube inside the bottle to take in the liquid.

The tube may clog up between sprayings and a little wire will clear it up. If your model to be sprayed is flat, keep it flat when you spray it; if it is a small statue keep it standing and spray over the liquid evenly. As described on Directions No. 1 you must allow the previous coating to set before you apply the successive ones. In fact you follow the same rule from now on. The difference is that instead of applying with brush you apply with sprayer. In fact after the first sprayer application you could use brush for others. The advantage of the first spraying being to avoid air bubble on the mold. It is a matter of preference with the worker, sprayer or brush. Brush is easier.

The length of time between applications for drying can be suggested as when the Rubber has turned to a darker red. If you work in a warm place it will set quicker—approximately twenty or thirty minutes would be a fair guess. Do not allow too long a time between the sprays as the rubber will not make a solid coating.

GELATINE CASTING

If you have a tray, a Jesso plaque, a bust, a vase, a small figure, and so on, that you want to reproduce, follow the instructions given here.

Take the article to be reproduced and wrap it up in thin tissue paper. This is done to prevent its being soiled during the process. Place it down on a board and if the article is flat smear its edges touching the board with cup grease, to keep it fast on the board, as otherwise it might float.

Now take some clay or Plastine; **Plastine** is a composition clay that remains soft. It can be used again and again. Now make a little wall around the article, being careful that it comes at least as high as the article itself or over. A strip of tin can be used and tied around the model.

Make some flat strips of the same clay and cover the article entirely with about one-third inch of the clay. This covering is connected with the wall around, and it makes a solid and holeproof coating. Smooth this clay coating with the hand or a knife.

Over this clay coating apply a good brushing of Plumer Candle and Kerosene, melted together. Over this you pour the Plaster of Paris; **Plaster of Paris** is poured in a bowl of water little by little until the powder shows above the surface of the water. Stir well and pour, which should have been stirred up thoroughly and made as thick as cream. Pour this over and over, making at least a one-inch (1-inch) shell all around. Now, smooth it up with a spatula or knife, and allow it to set about thirty minutes.

At the end of this period you lift it up from the board. You take out the article, and take out the clay. You now have a cavity between the article and the Jesso shell, caused by taking off the clay, and this cavity will be the space where the gelatine will be poured in later.

With a brush or rag clean the inside of the shell, and peel the paper wrapper from the model. Shellac the inside of the shell two times. If the model is not lacquered, it must also be shellacked well.

Now take a sharp pointed knife and dig a hole about one-half inch deep in the center part of the shell. After that, dig one small hole to the right and one to the left of the big hole. These two small holes are vents, while the large one in the center is to pour in the gelatine.

Place now the shell over the model, exactly in the center, but first fasten the model to the board with cup grease, to prevent the gelatine from going underneath and floating it. The plaster shell should be fastened to the board by plastine or clay, to prevent the gelatine from coming out.

Now you melt the gelatine glue. You may buy the regular gelatine at your grocer, Drug store or paint store who sell gelatine in powder quantity, according to the size of your cast. In a pail of water place an open-mouth jar. Pour into this a litt'e water, say five ounces, and let it come to a boil. In other words, the process is similar to that of a double-boiler. When the water boils in the jar pour in, spoon by spoon, about eight ounces of gelatine, in powder form, stirring constantly so that it will melt quickly. Keep on pouring and stirring until all of the gelatine is melted. Then take it off the fire and let it cool slightly, but not enough to become stiff, say ten minutes or so.

In the meantime you take a piece of clay and place it around the central hole in the shell, making it a kind of funnel. You now pour the liquid gelatine into this funnel, pouring very slowly, so as to give it time to flood the space inside the shell also to avoid air pockets. Keep on pouring until the space is filled up to the mouth. Gradually it will go down, and you refill it.

When full the two small holes at either side of the larger one, will give out some of the liquid. With a small piece of clay close up the two holes. This casting should be left undisturbed over night. In the morning you lift the plaster shell, you take off the model and there you find the exact form of the model enbossed in the gelatine. Plaster of Paris can now be poured in it, repeatedly, making a number of impressions. One impression requires about 30 minutes to set. The gelatine will finely deteriorate. It can be melted again and used anew.

Notice: There is made a **Molding Gelatine,** sold by the pound, which is placed in the double boiler, and will melt in about one-half hour.

Gelatine can be melted again and again. The work of molding should be done in a room where the temperature is not over 50 degree Fahrenheit, otherwise you must give your mold (on the inside) a good coat of varnish and when dry another coating. A coating of Raw linseed oil will be applied before you begin the molding.

SPLIT MOLD

No. 1 White

No. 2 Sprayed

No. 3—½ Shell

Split mold means a plaster shell made in two halves. While you can make a flat model with one shell, a statuette, a ball, or dog etc. must be made in 2 pieces or more. You have to spray or brush the model with rubber in the regular way to about one-sixteenth or one-eighth thickness, then you place a piece of tin around the model, leaving about one-half **inch** space between the statuette and the tin. This tin piece to cover the first half shell. You now pour the plaster of Paris in between the model and the tin and let it set. When the plaster is set, you make 4 holes on the shell to guide you in the 2nd half shell. The illustration No. 5 shown here gives an idea where to place these holes. You now proceed to make the other half of the shell, by placing the tin around the statuette No. 4 by pouring the plaster and let it set. Now you part the two pieces, and your shell is complete and ready for the casting.

It is often necessary to reproduce a statuette, a tall article etc. with protrduing parts, by making a split model, or a mold made in two pieces or more. I have made a few illustrations to show how this is done.

Take for instance the statuette No. 1. Cover it with life rubber in the regular way, either by brush or spray and brush (See instructions). No. 2. When very dry you now make a bed of clay, lay the statuette over the clay, and cover half of its roundness, (see illustration). Have a very straight and even clay edge about ¾″ wide.

It is understood that half of the figure is sunk into the clay and half is clear of the clay. See illustration No. 3. Now proceed to make a shell of plaster of Paris to the uncovered half part. Build up a wall of clay around the clay bed, about

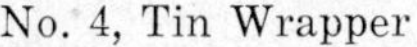

No. 4, Tin Wrapper

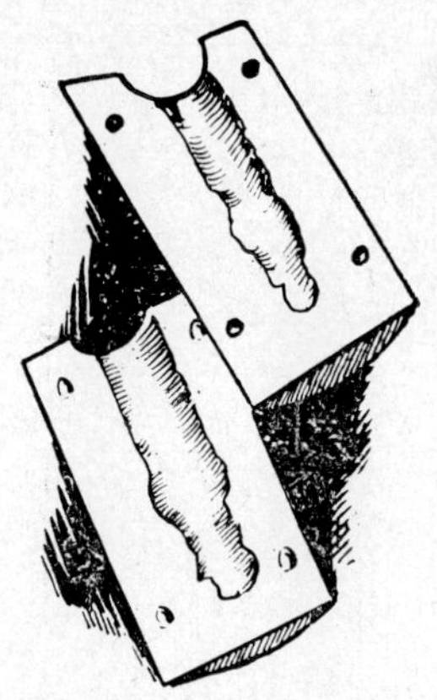

No. 5—2 ½ Shells

½ inch thick and high enough to be about 1 inch above the figure. This wall is to hold in check the plaster when you pour it over the figure. Cover the figure with olive oil to prevent it from attaching itself to the plaster. Make up your plaster and water mixture and pour it all over as high as the clay wall may allow you. Plaster will become warm and cool off in about 30 minutes. It is now time to lift off the whole block, take off all the clay sides and bottom and your figure will appear ½ imbedded in the plaster. Remove figure carefully and you now have ½ of the shell or mold alone. With a pointed knife you dig the 4 holes as shown in illustration 3 which will serve as keys to the 2nd ½ shell to be now made.

Replace figure on the first shell and oil it as before, then you build up the claywall again, one inch above the figure and proceed to pour the plaster mixture, freshly made, over the figure.

Instead of building the claywall you can use a piece of tin as shown on figure No. 5 and pour the plaster in, being certain that the bottom is tightly closed up with clay at the surface of the table. In about thirty minutes you can pry open the two half shells. We forgot to mention that the edge of the first shell where the keyholes are, must be oiled up very well otherwise you can't take them apart. As you now have the two shells complete take off the rubber coat from the statuette. Start from the bottom or pedestal, if any. Pull off just as you would try to pull off a robe you have on by taking it off from the bottom up through your head. This rubber shell is your master mold and is a perfect reproduction of your original figure. It should be open at the bottom. When you wish to make copies from this master mold, moisten its inside part with water, put it between the two half shells to fit smugly, tie the two half shells well and pour in the plaster-water mixture through the open bottom—until full. Allow about thirty minutes to dry, open up, peel off the rubber coat and you are ready for a second copy. This can be kept up and many reproductions can be turned out day after day.

HOW TO PREPARE PLASTER FOR THE CASTING

Take a bowl or any broad utensil of glass pottery, tin, wood, etc. As I don't know how large your cast is going to be I don't know how big this article must be. Let us say a small bust 6″ high. A quart of water is poured in the bowl, and well sifted plaster is slowly put into it until this powder protrudes from the water. Take now a wooden spoon or any flat piece and stir well until the mixture is smooth and as thick as thick cream. Pour it over the article, covering it entirely. Do not lose time in mixing the plaster after you have poured it into the water. Use a wooden spoon, or a flat piece of wood or your hands, and stir it clean of lumps. If you don't pour it now, it will set and you will not be able to do a good job. Plaster mixture will set in about 30 minutes. When it has cooled you can safely begin to take it off the model.

Plaster cast can be painted over direct, using water colors. If oil painting is to be used over them, they should be either shellaced or lacquered over before the painting. Oil colors can, when dry, be coated with clear varnish. If there is a relief frame around the plaque, that should be properly painted in gold bronze, or a clear oil color yellow to imitate gold.

X9—8x12

Flapper Girl. Use Flesh tint, **7c** tube, BLACK BACKGROUND. USE BRIGHT COLORS in flowers. Hat mauve. Hair, Raw Sienna. **75c.**

Silhouettes are generally painted in black on white or ivory color back ground. Ivory color can be made with white and little light chrome yellow. But of course any other color effect can be tried to suit your taste.

When you apply the life Rubber its color is a light **Rose-color** but when it dries and sets it becomes **Red**, almost like a poppy color. Then you reapply.

You must apply it several times before the required thickness of the Rubber is obtained. You can start and finish the mold within twelve hours or so. Start it in the morning and it will set well through the next night. This does not mean that you have to work twelve hours, only on the molding, as you could carry out half a dozen varied molds within this time. There is always a considerable pause between applications.

The thickness of the Rubber mold I give approximately at about the same thickness as a 25c silver piece.

⦿⦿⦿⦿⦿

CHAPTER I
Jesso Craft Art

JESSO CRAFT is the art of decorating beautiful plaques, screens, boxes and novelties by very simple methods and can be done at home. Any person, with good taste and average artistic ability, can easily learn to make distinctive gifts by following the instructions in this booklet. It is very fascinating work and many people are making money selling finished Jesso work or are teaching this craft. Especially in the small city or town there are many opportunities of forming classes in which you can teach Jesso craft and by following the instructions herein you should become quite proficient and capable of teaching in a short time.

CHAPTER II
Materials Needed for This Work

WE OUTLINE first necessary materials required with which to do this work. The cost is little and usually many articles can be made from the materials or outfit you first purchase. The most important article used in Jesso craft is the paste or clay which is employed for the purpose of building up, working out, or finishing up the article you desire to make. There are many kinds of clay on the market, but not all of them are good, some have been found gritty, others will not harden and again some will crack after they have hardened with the result that your work will fall away. So it is essential to use a good clay or paste, one that spreads smoothly and will stand up well and dry quickly. (From experience it was found that the Jesso paste prepared by D. M. Campana Art Company, Chicago, gave the best result and it cannot be equaled.) Jesso paste or clay is a preparation composed of several ingredients of which we give the formula in this book, which when dried will form a heavy background in stippled or mottled effect and likewise a composition frame to the article on which it is applied. In additional to the already prepared clay sold in cans it is now possible to obtain "dry" clay in powder form. This is simply mixed in lukewarm water and then applied over the article to be decorated in the manner as you apply the clay in the can, however, the surface of any object to which it is applied must first be sized or shellacked.

The mixture is applied flat, just brushed on smooth with a wide brush and after it has "set" for three hours it can be stippled by daubing the surface with a rang or a stubby bristle brush.

You may decorate all shapes of articles, but without question the wood panels are the most popular. They can be purchased in many shapes and sizes, prices varying from 12 cents for a small plaque to 75 cents and higher for larger plaques, depending on the construction. It is also possible to buy the plaques in what is called compo board, this article being made of heavy cardboard, however the wood panels are best suited for Jesso work. Telephone screens, novelty boxes, handkerchief boxes, book ends, wall scones, fire screens, swing easels and numerous other articles all can be worked up in the Jesso craft method. We show in this book a few illustrations of articles which are very popular.

In addition to the clay and the above articles, the other materials are brushes, colors and colored pictures; composition ornaments are now also being used extensively and further on we shall explain more about these. As for the brushes only two or three are necessary usually two for applying the paste and these should be a stiff bristle preferably round and short, one small, one large. In addition a brush is also necessary to apply your color later on over the clay to complete the color scheme of the article you make up. Colored pictures, prints or transfers are all necessary to have, for it it around these that the objects are decorated in the Jesso clay. Complete outfits containing a full assortment of materials for Jesso work can also be purchased for about $3.50.

The size of the center picture depends upon the size of plaque or box, yet it should be placed so that it will be in balance with the rest of the work you put on the article. Colored prints suitable for this work can be purchased from 10 cents to $1.00 according to the size. Usually studies with abundant colors are more suitable, for these will tend to add to the attractiveness of the finished article. Get a study of the correct proportion to the plaque and study this matter before you attempt to glue it down. We illustrate in this booklet numerous studies suitable for this work. Note the studies on some of the finished plaques that are shown here.

Colors Used in Jesso Craft

As for colors the most popular for use in this work are the bronze powder colors and you will find that most Jesso craft articles are finished with these. Bronze colors can be had in several colors and usually when several or even numerous plaques are to be made up it is advisable to purchase a full assortment of these, that is at least twelve colors and the bronzing medium in which they are mixed. A full assortment of twelve colors, brushes, liquid, etc., cost about $3.00.. To use these colors you pour out a small amount of the bronzing liquid in a saucer and add a little of the desired shade of bronze powder to this, just thick enough to about the consistency of cream, mix well in the liquid and apply quickly as it will thicken within a short time.

Good landscapes, marines, birds, etc., with
plenty colors make the most attractive plaques.
Write the author for free list.

Oil colors or water colors are also used. The primary colors
are red, yellow, blue, green, brown, black, white and with these
you can produce any other color by mixing these in the proper
proportions.

From these colors a very complete combination and any
desired effect may be secured as we show you in the following
chart:

Orange — Mix red and yellow. Vary the proportions to se-
sure shade you wish. For gray orange use three parts orange
to one part blue. Violet — Mix blue and red. Equal parts will
make a vivid violet. Change proportions to suit tone desired.
For gray violet use three parts violet to one part yellow.
Greens — As green is made up of yellow and blue, you can
vary the green by adding yellow for lighter or moss green
tone. Add blue to deepen the green. For gray green mix three
parts green to one part red. Reds — Mix with white for pink
shades. To make old rose, mix red and white with a little
yellow and blue. Maroon red, or deep red mix in brown as desired. Gray red, mix three parts red to one part green. Yellow
— Add red to make orange yellow, green to make yellow
green, black to make dark yellow. For gray yellow mix three
parts yellow to one part violet. Blues — Add white to make
lighter or pale blue — black to make darker shades. Add yellow to give a greenish cast. Gray blue is made by mixing three
parts blue to one part orange. Brown — This is a mixture of
orange and green. Vandyke Brown is a dark shade and is sold
under this name. To make lighter brown or tan add orange
or yellow as desired. Add red to make maroon brown.

This is a simple plaque to make. The outside edge of the plaque has a plain wood strip glued onto it, extending ¼ inch higher than the board. The inner frame has a double row of wood strip set up ¼ inch from the board. Plain stippling.

CHAPTER III
Making a Jesso Craft Plaque
(Using a colored picture)

ASSUMING that you have before you the wood panel, clay, picture, brushes, etc., let us proceed to finish up or construct the plaque. Work on a clean table, have plenty or room and proceed carefully. First let us say again that we think it always advisable to shellac the surface of the object you wish to decorate.

The picture is the famous "Daybreak" by Maxfield Parrish. The ornaments at each side and bottom are composition Jesso ornaments. The design at top of plaque was modeled with clay and the balance of the plaque is in rough stipple. The inner frame around the print is in bright gold, the ornaments also, while the stippling is colored in umber.

CHAPTER IV
Mounting the Picture

HAVE a little library paste or glue handy. First place the print face down on a clean piece of paper and with a brush distribute water evenly over the back. Allow no free water to remain, but immediately brush paste or glue evenly over the whole dampened surface. Now place the picture on the plaque and be sure to center it. (It would be best to find the center of the plaque and sort of measure just where to place the picture.) Press picture down firmly until paste or glue sets. Allow to dry for short while and if you have some furniture wax rub this over the print which will waterproof the surface. (This could not be done to original paintings, sketches, charcoal or water color pictures without first setting the colors, which is done by applying fixatif or special light picture varnish, but can easily be done over a print.) Rub the wax gently with a clean cloth and remove excess wax. If the plaque has an inner frame you place the picture herein and waterproof in the same way as explained. In illustration No. 1 we show how the print has been applied to center of the plaque and is now ready for the clay.

Illustration No. 1

This shows how the colored print is pasted down in the center of the plaque.

CHAPTER V
Applying Ornaments and Paste

MAKE at first a little frame close to the print to give it more striking effect. This little frame can be done by applying the Jesso paste over and over until you have a sufficient thickness and height, say about ¼ inch. This takes considerable time and is difficult, and better and quicker work can be done by using a rope well tacked down with small nails. It is afterward covered with Jesso clay and looks good. Another way is to pin on strips of wood, purposely made and sold and those are also covered with Jesso clay. I also suggest you build up any ornament on the upper part of the plaque or at the side and bottom, using ornaments or strips and procede afterwards with the background. In applying any wood strips

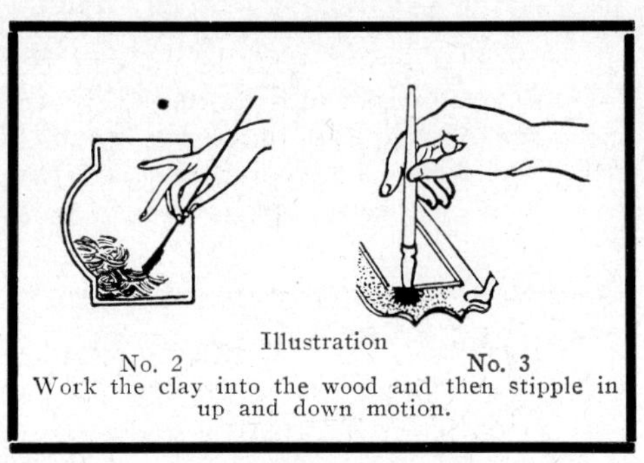

Illustration

Work the clay into the wood and then stipple in
up and down motion.

or ornaments it is advisable to glue them on and further nail them down with fine short nails which will be easily covered with the Jesso paste.

Proceed now to scoop up with your bristle brush a quantity of the Jesso paste and apply to the surface beyond the print. Now work the clay into the wood and then stipple it with a short up and down motion, holding the brush in a vertical position. (See illustration 2-3.) Other effective stipple designs may be made by rolling the brush head almost horizontally or by using a circular twist with the brush head vertically. The clay must be applied heavily, even the edges of the plaque must be covered. If there is an inner frame or any moulding on the plaque, as in illustration 1, this also should be covered lightly with clay. It will require from three to 12 hours for the clay to dry. If you then feel the first application of the paste is not sufficiently high apply second coat of paste. In other words, this clay can be reapplied over the first coating so as to make the decoration higher.

Sandpapering the Plaque

When the clay is thoroughly dry take a piece of fine sandpaper and rub lightly over the entire surface, being careful, however, not to injure the picture in the center. This will remove all hard edges and points. Now brush off all the dust, using a clean dry brush or cloth. It is now ready for coloring.

CHAPTER VI
Coloring

FIRST cut out a piece of stiff cardboard the size of the print in the center of the plaque. This is needed to protect the picture from being smeared with the color. As stated heretofore, bronze colors are mostly used, likewise oil colors, the latter to give an antique finish. We will explain both.

(A)   Take about a teaspoonful of the gold bronze powder and mix this with the bronzing liquid to about the consistency of cream. You need not necessarily use gold as copper, green and orange are also good colors suitable for this work. The gold, however, is mostly used. Now protect the print with the cardboard and with a soft camel-hair brush apply the bronze color all over. See illustration.

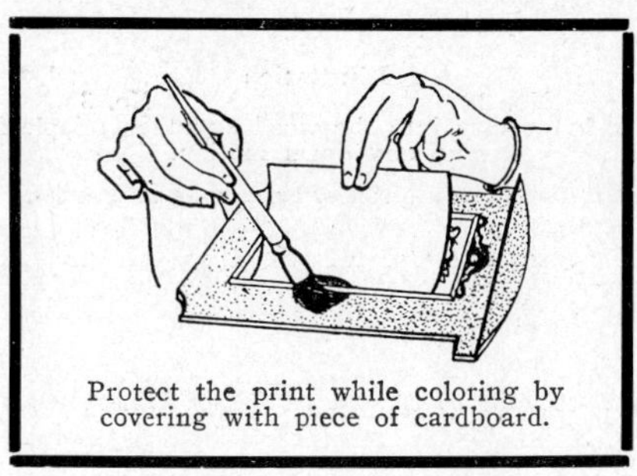

Protect the print while coloring by covering with piece of cardboard.

Be sure to cover well, in fact, a second application is advisable. When this is dry you can, if you wish, daub a little of the green bronze powder here and there which will give it the green gold effect. These bronze powders can be varied one over the other — it is all a matter of taste, but they should harmonize to a certain extent with the color in the picture. The bronze colors will dry in 30 minutes.

(B)   You may prefer to give the plaque the old-fashioned artistic set-off. This is accomplished with oil colors but they are applied over the gilded or bronze gold surface, or vice versa. Remember you must first apply gold bronze color and let this dry for 30 minutes. To use now the oil colors, first bear in mind that you select the colors best adapted to the tone and subject of the picture. You then mix these with a little turpentine and then paint over the gilded surface and allow it to settle for a few minutes, then rub the antiqued surface with an old cotton rag which will absorb most of the color from the high spots. Now a second color can be effectively added, daubing this in spots, brown on blue, blue on gray, blue on brown, etc. Distribute the spots unevenly in circles of one-half inch in diameter. Blot the spots lightly with a cloth and then rub evenly over surface. Now a final operation is to rub rotten-stone over the clay, but this is not essential, it just tends to give the colors the dull appearance. In this connection we might add that the high spots where gold appears through can be burnished with an agate which will brighten up the gold. The agate must be heated for proper results. A plain finished plaque will look like illustration shown as "Finished Plain Plaque."

Plain stippled finish plaque.

Italian Renaissance Finish

When the clay is dry, cover the entire surface with gold so that no white spots show up. Let the gold dry for at least an hour. Then cover the entire surface with a coat of brown oil paint, any shade desired. Take a cloth and rub this paint off high spots immediately and by rubbing down with the gold showing through gives you a very good effect. If desired the entire clay surface can be polished with floor wax.

CHAPTER VII
How to Make Different Articles
How to Make a Screen in Jesso Craft

THERE are many different shapes and styles of screens. There are telephone screens, fire screens, boudoir screens, etc., but we will outline here how to make up one of the small telephone screens. This screen is hinged and as there are three sections one must take into consideration that three panels must be completed. See illustration.

The center panel is, of course, the primary panel and the most important and requires the most work. Here is where we place the print. Usually it is best to get a subject showing an object in the center surrounded with flowers, shrubbery, water, etc., so that the picture can be cut in three sections using the center for the primary panel and the balance of the picture placed in the side panels of the screen to harmonize (see illustration of screen).

It is not essential to use the large picture as a picture only in the center panel with plain stippling on the side panel may be preferred by many. Carry out the stippling and coloring the same as you would do on a plaque, as mentioned in previous chapters.

Showing how the water effect is
carried out in the side panels.

Wooden Boxes and Treasure Chest

In these boxes you have a large assortment to choose
from. Many firms sell these boxes in various shapes and sizes.
Some are used as handkerchief boxes, jewel boxes, sewing
boxes, etc., and all make splendid gifts and useful articles for
the home. On these boxes the decoration is more or less a
matter of taste, some may prefer to use a small colored print,
others prefer just a border around the edge of stippled Jesso
paste set in relief leaving the balance of the box in smooth
Jesso finish and when dry, color it. On a treasure chest, for
example, if you wish to use a colored picture you can purchase
a small print, preferably a floral subject, and use this across the
concave top of the treasure chest and along the front. Glue it
down firmly the same as you would on a plaque. With the use
of a little strong twine about one-eighth inch in thickness
make a sort of border around the picture glueing down the
twine with strong glue. Make a light pencil line to show where
your border is to be placed and then run the twine as evenly
as possible and glue down the twine over the pencil line. When
this is dry cover all with your Jesso paste, protecting the print.
Cover the twine as heavily as you wish, this to act as a frame.
Stipple sides, front and back. When thoroughly dry proceed
to color as described in preceeding pages. If you prefer to have
the picture on the front of the chest, place it in the center and
follow up with the work as described above.

On low, flat boxes the colored print always will look best
on the top, the balance of the box can be covered with Jesso
paste and colored. You can carry out the idea of putting a
frame all around the box if you wish by glueing down twine
about one-quarter inch away from the edge of the front, back

and side and then cover all over with Jesso paste. Further on the method of working up relief designs in Jesso paste is explained.

Candlesticks and Vases

On candlesticks and slender, narrow vases you have not enough surface for use of a colored picture. Here we apply just the Jesso paste, stippling lightly so as to give a sort of a hammered effect. On candlesticks we can give the two-tone effect in the coloring by using the oil colors over the paste and coloring the base of the candlestick in one color and the upper in another. You may prefer bright colors in which case a combination of bright red and green will prove attractive. Of course you must purchase wax ornamental candles which will harmonize in color with the candlesticks. Other color schemes can be carried out in similar ways. If you prefer just the gold candlesticks apply the rich gold bronze powder all over the surface and if you have an agate, use this to burnish as we have explained heretofore. Vases can be decorated in similar ways but an effort should be made to blend one color into the other, i. e., start with a deep color at the top and shade down to pale at the bottom.

Book Ends

Book ends are always useful in the home and many people are working these up in Jesso craft. There are several ways to decorate these and further on we explain additional methods of decoration. This is the simplest way. Book ends require a small print, but you must have two prints alike. A picture of a ship, marine scene or girl head always shows up well on book ends. Do not show too large a picture for it will tend to spoil the balance of the work. If you have a picture which you think is too large you can trim it down to a size that will be appropriate. Glue both prints down firmly on the face or front of the book ends. Polish up the print with wax as described heretofore. Here you can make use of a Jesso paste bulb if you have one. Draw a pencil line around the picture and then with your Jesso bulb full of paste squeeze out the paste along the pencil line. Do not squeeze out too much but just make sort of a narrow ribbon around the print. If you do not have a Jesso bulb you could get one of those cake decorating sets made of rubber to form a cone and put the Jesso paste therein. There is also a little article of this kind sold at the 5 and 10 cent store. It is useful for many things. The balance of the book end is then finished in the Jesso paste, whichever way you wish to work it in. Do not fail to cover the back of the book end and the top and sides. Color in bronze or give antique finish by using oils.

CHAPTER VIII

Modeling With Jesso — Working Up Designs in Relief

JESSO modeling is an old art revived and when applied in Jesso Craft produces fascinating and beautiful effects. In this work no colored print is used, but rather you must first model your subject on the article you wish to decorate and later color the finished model in oil or water colors, similar to making a regular painting. In this work you purchase the plaque, screen or box, whichever you wish to make up. You also purchase a colored picture, to be used as a model to work from, of a subject that can be decorated in bright colors, i. e., a study of a parrot or a cardinal bird, marine or ship scene, etc. The study will have to be in proportion to the size of the article you wish to make up. With the aid of piece of tracing paper trace an outline of the subject in the study on the tracing paper. Use pen and ink to make the outline or tracing good and clear. When you have this take a piece of carbon paper, lay this below the tracing and place on the plaque or screen, whichever you will work up. Be sure you place the tracing or outline in the center and now, with a hard-pointed pencil, follow the pen lines, making up the form of the subject. By this we mean just the outside lines, no need to trace outline of features — this can be done later.

You can now commence to lay in your Jesso paste. The purpose is to set the subject in high relief, so fill in the clay thickly and try to keep it smooth.

With a modeling tool or a stick try to model out of this surface the subject you are copying. If it is a parrot, carve out some of the feathers, the eye, the beak, claws, etc. If it is a flower, carve out some of the petals, the leaves, stems, etc.

If you do not get it high enough you can add more when the first application is dry. You can then proceed to stipple the rest of the plaque; just one covering with paste will suffice; also be sure to cover edges. After you have finished let the clay dry for a day. Then smooth down with fine sandpaper the rough edges on your figure in the center. Try to get this as smooth as possible. The next step is to retouch and reapply Jesso paste if higher relief is desired, giving as much detail as you can. You are now ready to color. You have the study showing the subject in colors, so follow the color scheme as close as possible with oil color. You may find that in using some clay the oil color will be taken up by the clay, leaving a matt finish, but this can be brightened up later by using light varnish. It is also advisable sometimes to give the clay a light coat of shellac before coloring. Now as for the background, this can be colored to suit your taste. You may prefer bronze color or oil color, but in all cases use a color that will harmonize with the model in the center. For example, if you have modeled a parrot and have finished this in various bright colors, the background could be finished in black or dark blue. If your model is a ship scene, then the background should represent water and waves, putting in occasional dabs of white for wave effect.

When a dragon is used as a model the background had best be in rich gold, the dragon in green, gold and black, etc. At this point we wish to mention that one can use Campana's Enamelite colors, just as well as oil colors. The enamelite colors will dry with a glossy surface. The plaque when finished should be hung with silk cords and tie, choosing a color that will harmonize with the colors in the plaque.

Book Ends, Boxes, Etc.

These are made up similar to the plaques. On book ends the addition of a modeled border around your subject will add to the appearance. A good effect can be obtained by modeling a floral spray from Permadello Clay. This will dry very hard and the flowers will be in high relief. When book ends are finished glue heavy felt on the bottom.

On boxes such as handkerchief boxes, etc., your model should, of course, be on top of the boxes, but it is also well to add a little decoration on the front and even sides. Supposing the model on top showed a floral spray then the same or similar idea should be carried out on the front of the box but smaller in size. On a round box the simplest way is best to confine your model to top only. If the model is a conventional design a circle made of clay around it will set it off nicely. From the circle to the edge you can give the stipple effect, likewise all around the side of the box.

On telephone screens you can place model on center panel, make this in proportion to the size of panel, stipple all around model and stipple side likewise. To give whirl effect use wide brush dragging paste on in half circular motion of the hand. Many attractive subjects for screens, book ends and small articles can be obtained from hot iron patterns.

These are outlines which can be transferred to the article by running a hot iron over the design. There is a great variety of these patterns and they are sold by the full sheet containing many designs, for 30 cents. For elaborate Jesso modeling, illustration No. 8 gives the reader an idea of design built up entirely in Jesso and then colored in oils and bronzes.

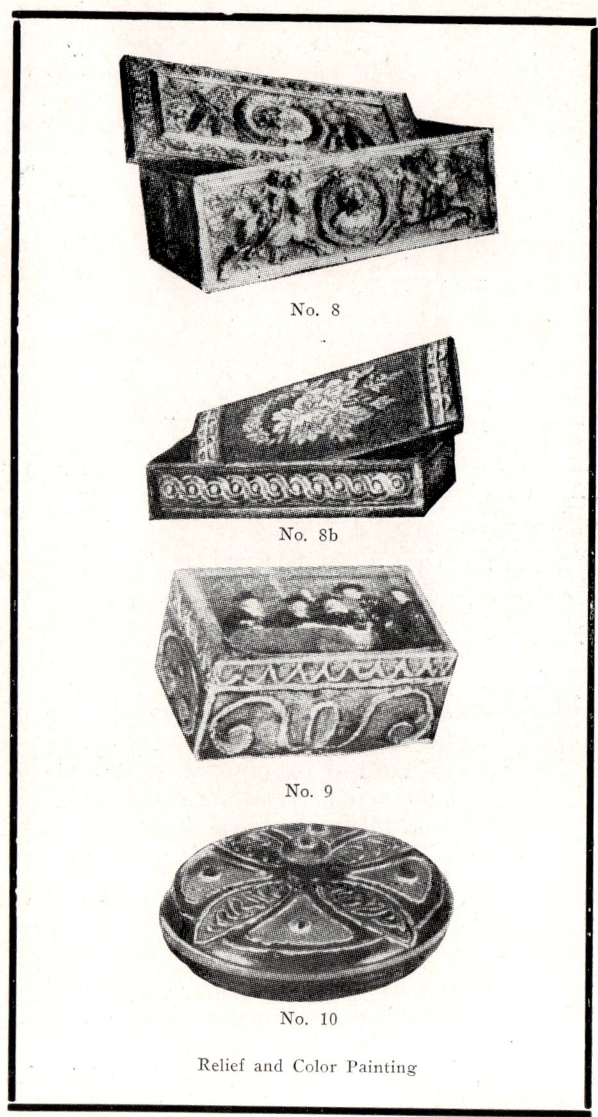

No. 8

No. 8b

No. 9

No. 10

Relief and Color Painting

In illustration 8B we show how the use of a Jesso ornament on the front and sides has added to its attractiveness.

In illustrations No. 9 and 10 we illustrate various shapes of boxes and show how the decoration is applied.

On boxes an attractive way to decorate these is to run a border of flowers around the edge of the box, possibly one-half inch wide. Just a little spray of two or three flowers, then a space, then another spray until you are around the box. It is best to draw an even line around so that the border will be even all around. The center can then be left plain and sides also. This is all a matter of taste. It is from experience that we quote these suggestions and hints.

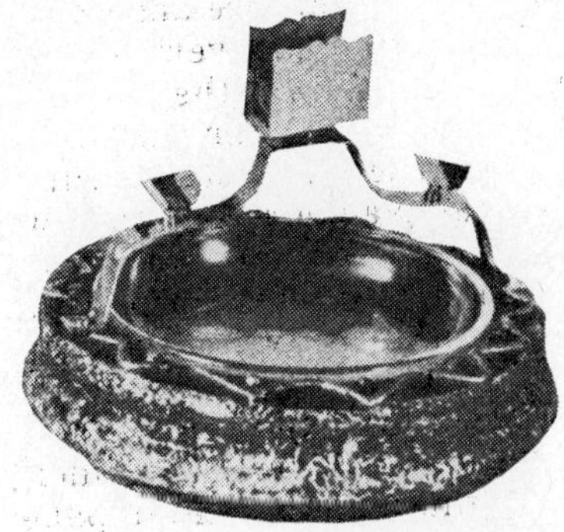

The ash tray shows all-over hammered effect, obtained by fine stippling of the Jesso paste. The design at top was made with rope, covered with clay.

CHAPTER IX
Jesso Ornaments and Their Use - See Page 35

JESSO ornaments are made up of special composition poured into a molded design and hardened. They are very attractive and in addition to using them in Jesso Craft they can be used on furniture and for any other ornamental purposes. In using them on some articles there is no other decoration excepting that light stippling is necessary. There are numerous designs in ornaments made in just the proper size for use on all articles and we illustrate many different ones on the following page. In the catalog of D. M. Campana Art Company, Chicago, Illinois, you will find a selection of ornaments suitable for all purposes. Jesso ornaments are supplied in dry state and when you receive such ornaments it will be necessary to soften them first before using. This is best done by placing them between the folds of a very wet towel and leave them for at least four hours or longer. This will soften the composition so that they can then be easily applied to all objects and generally to all surfaces. The ornaments are glued or nailed down with fine nails and when dry you then stipple the entire balance of the piece with a light covering of clay, and likewise go over the ornament very lightly with a little of clay. This is, however, only a suggestion. Do not stretch or pull the ornament longer than its original size in order to cover a certain space — if you do the ornament will shrink in drying and crack in several places. The ornament need not necessarily be covered. Then you will have to give the ornament a light covering of white shellac and when dry, paint up the ornament in your oil or bronze colors. The color scheme is more or less a matter of taste and naturally depends upon the design itself.

In coloring the ornament with bronze powder colors touch up the high spots with the gold. The background can be colored in oil or bronze, but one single color here will suffice and usually when left in a matt finish the decorations are very attractive. In using the Jesso ornaments on a plaque they can be used as a decorative heading just above the picture or model in the center. Ornaments can be purchased in a set of three pieces, one piece being placed across the plaque at top and two corresponding pieces dropping from the sides part way down the plaque just between the edges and the picture. The ornaments are given one coloring, usually one that will harmonize with color in the picture or model. The background of the plaque is finished in the antique finish as explained in preceeding pages. Now on a telephone screen a Jesso ornament is very useful for the side panels. In the main or center panel you can put your colored picture or your model and then in each side panel glue down an ornament that will correspond with the dimensions of the panel. Usually a slender ornament placed in the center looks best and you then stipple all around. Likewise on boxes, assuming you have a printed picture at the top, you can place a narrow ornament along the front of the box, color it and stipple in your background with clay. And so in many other articles the addition of these ornaments will at all times aid to the attractiveness and appearance of the piece. They are useful in helping you give it the finished appearance, lends to its selling value and takes away the amateurish effect.

Building Ornaments

There are several ways in which one can build up the object to get the decorative effect. Wood strips, from one-eighth inch thickness up are used to good advantage to enable you to work up a border, frame, etc., and likewise for making other decorative effects on the object you work up in Jesso. To make oval, curved and round borders and for other similar purposes one can use reed and bamboo strips of small diameter. These are very flexible and can be bent or turned without fear of

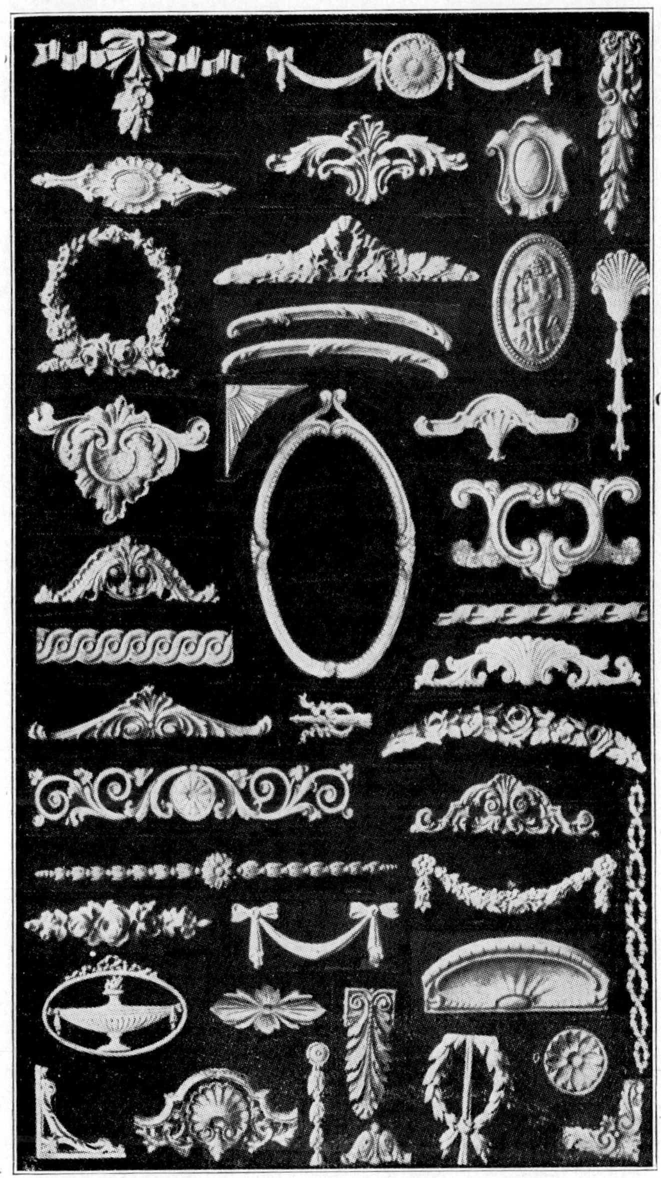

One has a great variety of Jesso ornaments to choose from.

cracking them. They should be tacked down with small wire nails and also held down with strong glue. Strips of rope of different thicknesses can also be used. The Jesso paste is then applied over the strips. These strips can be bought for a few cents each in varied lengths. Another way to make up your own ornamental designs is to use cardboard cutouts. You can take any plain design which you think will look nice on the piece you intend to work up and trace this on a piece of heavy cardboard, preferably one-eighth inch thick, and then cut this out with a sharp knife. You then place on the article to be decorated. The cardboard ornament must also be held down with glue and the Jesso paste is then put over the cardboard ornament, and it is then painted.

Speaking of ornaments shown on previous page. A person with a little sense of art can copy those pretty designs and apply them on any decoration. Make them with clay and allow drying. Then if you make the mold you can sell them.

CHAPTER X

Useful Hints and Helpful Suggestions

FOR rough stipple surface dab fresh coated Jesso paste with a small wad of crumpled paper. This will produce an irregular raised surface. For woven effect or basket weave background apply thin coat of paste and while fresh work into checks, alternating perpendicular and horizontal with a small strip of cardboard about three-eighths of an inch wide. Sandpaper off imperfections. To produce inlaid designs, pearl chips may be set into design by glueing them onto a given spot first using strong glue. When thoroughly dry spread Jesso around and slightly over the edge of these and model the remainder of the design.

Artificial fruit and flowers, etc., may be glued onto baskets and box lid and finished with Jesso. After you have glued these down firmly and glue has dried, paint the flower petals or leaves with white shellac and permit to harden. If desired you can purchase already complete glazed artificial flowers, etc., and use these. Coat them with Jesso paste to give a hard modeled finish. The round knob on a box lid may be converted into a rose by glueing petals of cotton rose about and finishing it off with Jesso paste, or you can use the petals of an artificial cloth rose or build up around the knob and model with Jesso paste. In order to obtain drip effect on candlesticks make long drippings of the Jesso paste along the finished surface and background.

To obtain a nice smooth surface apply your Jesso paste and then smooth this surface, while paste is still soft, by dipping a flat knife or a palette knife in water and going over the surface for a second time just as if you were smoothing the icing on a cake. You can also smooth up your freshly applied work by going over it again and again with a water-filled brush.

You can also make a picture frame of Jesso paste in the following way: Obtain from a stationery store a sheet of heavy cardboard at least one-eighth inch thick and with a sharp knife cut this in strips the size of the frame you wish to make. Take strong glue and glue these strips down, one, or perhaps two over the other, until you get the desired height. Bind together with adhesive tape so as to hold the pieces securely together. You will need four sides to complete your frame, so cut all the necessary strips for all sides. Remember that you must mitre the corners, meaning the corners must be cut on a slant, so that the other side will fit tightly against it, and all the corners must be glued tightly together. Even the addition of a few small nails through the corners will help to secure them and hold them together firmly. When your cardboard frame is completed you can either stipple this plain or, if you wish, cut a narrow strip of cardboard, say one-eighth of an inch wide, and glue this down all around the center of the frame and when dry cover all over with Jesso paste. You can also use a cord if you wish to give the center of the frame a rounded effect. The cord should also be one-eighth inch in thickness and glued down. Draw first a center line all around so that you will get the cord on evenly. Apply clay all over the cord in smooth surface, the rest of the frame you can put in stipple effect. When dry apply covering of gold bronze color. When this is complete you will have to take a plain piece of heavy cardboard and glue or nail it down over the entire back of the frame. On this you later lay your colored picture and over this the glass. The glass can be held in place by tacking down narrow strips of wood (which are to be bronzed) over the edge of the glass and into the side of the frame itself. Remember this is the last operation.

Another suggestion we might mention is that in cutting the different strips of cardboard which go into making the frame, four of the strips, making sides, top and bottom, be cut one-fourth inch wider than the other and this strip then placed in the center of the other strips and all glued together. When the frame is finished you can get a piece of glass to fit the frame and insert the glass from the back so that it rests against this extension. Your printed picture is then placed

against the glass and to hold all this take a heavy piece of
cardboard and push into the frame from the back this all
being held in place by nailing in several of the small wire nails
into the side of the frame and extending over the cardboard
back.

Four-piece desk set finished in Jesso. Designs have been
modeled.

Here is an easy way to make a pretty desk set. You will
need a good heavy piece of cardboard at least three-sixteenths
of an inch thick. A good piece of compo board will do, but it
must be size 15x20 or larger; also two extra strips, each about
three and one-fourth inches wide. Glue the strips down on the
large board at each side, using good strong glue and put a
heavy weight on them to hold them down firmly. The next
think to do is to find a suitable little design to put on these
sides. Trace the design thereon and then fill in with Jesso
paste. After it is dry stipple lightly the balance, and then later
color in oils. You can buy large desk blotters to cover top of
the cardboard and you might also cover the entire bottom with
green or red felt. At the stationery store you can purchase
desk accessories, such as calendar pad, inkwell, stamp box, etc.,
and also these can be worked over in Jesso paste and then
painted to correspond with the colors in the desk pad.

Even crockery bowls, etc., can be artistically worked over
in Jesso. You can purchase at the 5 and 10 cent store ordinary
bowls, either in crockery or glass, but select an attractive
shape. Apply a covering of Jesso paste to the outer surface,
working this in a scroll effect. Decorate in bronze and color
as you please and you will find that at practically no cost you
have created an ornament that may be used acceptably in your
home. In addition, a coat of enamelite on the inside of the bowl
gives an additional pleasing effect. Should the bowl be of
glass, cover the outside with enamelite and when dry apply
the Jesso paste. The color will show through to the inside.
Flower pots, glass or tin vases can all be decorated in Jesso
paste and you will be surprised at the attractive articles you
can produce.

Another important hint is in regards to the Jesso ornaments, which we mention again. These, as you receive them are very brittle and must be handled carefully. Before using them it is necessary to soften them and this is easily accomplished by placing the ornaments between the folds of a wet towel. After leaving them here for three or four hours they become flexible and are easily glued down or a small nail can be driven through them. On account of the flexibility you can also apply them to a rounded or concave surface. Always use good strong furniture glue for fastening them down. Even if the ornament happens to be broken you can still use it, for after softening the ends can be tightly joined together and the break will never show.

If your Jesso paste is too heavy the addition of a little warm water will thin it out quickly. After you are through working with the paste put the cover on tightly, otherwise the paste will harden. All your brushes and articles used in Jesso work can be washed and cleaned in warm water.

CHAPTER XI

Polychrome Wax Objects

POLYCHROME wax is used mostly for the delicate modeling of flowers, fruits, leaves, lines, etc. It is especially adapted to plaques and picture frames. It is thicker than the clay and can be molded with the fingers. It is important always to keep the wax warm when using. This is done by placing the can in a bowl of hot water and renewing the water as it gets cold. After putting an undercoat of clay on the article to be decorated, and allowing it to harden, place some talcum powder in a little dish into which the fingers may be dipped if the wax is sticky. Take a small piece of the wax in your fingers and mold your design, a rose, a bunch of grapes, or whatever it may be. The petals of a flower are molded separately and stuck together by moistening the center ends with a little water and when the design is complete, it must be glued onto the clay covered article. The clay and wax process finished, you proceed in the same way with the gold and brown or blue and silver and the touches of color. An old mirror frame that has lost its personality may be successfully rejuvenated by removing the old varnish, sand papering the frame and applying a coat of the magic clay. You can buy Jesso ornaments and corner designs to glue on, and when they are covered with gold and a touch of color, look almost like hand carvings. The glass itself if not in good shape, can be resilvered at very small expense and behold a brand new, useful, decorative piece of furniture.

This plaque represents a medallion. The circle around picture is colored in dark vandyke brown, balance in gold. The scroll design was made with the use of cord, glued down, covered with clay and then colored.

CHAPTER XII
Valance Boards Made Up in Jesso Craft

FOR many homemakers, fine valance boards are the ultimate touch in furnishing that the household budget just cannot achieve. Placed over windows or doorways they will be found extremely effective in settling off your drapes, curtains or portierres. The materials needed for this work are similar to those used for making plaques. You can use either two-ply veneer panel, which must be thoroughly dry or regular compo or wall board, but be sure it has a good, smooth surface. The board should be cut the exact width of the window or door frame for which the valance is to be used. Some of the boards may be cut out in design and by making a pattern showing how it is to be cut any friend who has a scroll saw can cut this out for you, or you can purchase a small scroll saw for 50 cents. Do not make the valance too deep or you will spoil the appearance of the drapes; usually these vary from six to ten inches in depth. Jesso ornaments can well be used on these as well as prints. The object is to color the valance to harmonize with your drapes or curtains, and to get good color effect. Regular enamel color can be used over the Jesso clay instead of the bronze or oil colors. Especially in a sun room or sleeping porch where drapes are of cretonnes very colorful valances can be made to match the color scheme.

The board may also be finished in with wood stains for simple effects, then with dashing color of paint or textile to make it gay. On plain curtains the valance can be made with a graceful drop line above the curtains and then colored in delicate shades and by placing a silhouette motif in the center makes it very effective. Patterns for various valances can be obtained through the Woman's Home Companion at reasonable prices.

CHAPTER XIII

Sealing Wax Plaques

AS IN Jesso Craft sealing wax is used in making plaques with raised designs in high relief. Unusual effects can be obtained and because of the fact that they are built up from a printed design, one need not necessarily be able to draw to accomplish very charming and artistic results. Floral, birds and similar designs are the most popular and easiest to make. The foundation or plaque itself can be either a veneer panel, heavy cardboard, compo board, etc., cut to the desired shape. In addition you will need an assortment of sticks of sealing wax; usually twelve gives a good variety of colors. Also an alcohol lamp and a small palette knife. Some stationery and department stores carry a complete outfit especially for this work. The publisher of this book will send you free complete list.

Working Up the Plaque

The background is always covered first. It is usually a dark color such as black, dark green or dark blue, as this will give contrast and will help to bring out the brighter colors in your design. Heat the end of the stick of wax until it is just ready to drop, then jot it down quickly on the plaque holding the stick in a perpendicular position. Do this until the entire surface is covered. Be sure that the daubs of wax are close enough together so that the entire surface is covered.

Now cut out your design and paste down carefully over this surface. Suitable designs can be cut from decorated crepe wall paper, magazine pictures, etc. You now cover this paper design with your sealing wax using the same colors as those which appear in the printed design. Have the wax quite thick on the design so that it is well raised from the background. Add the colors to be used for shading last. Flowers are molded while wax is still warm and sometimes the addition of a drop of a little darker wax of the same shade will add toward giving it color. The flower can be shaped by following the design, and detail can be obtained by smoothing down or cutting in on the wax while it is still warm. Shading can be made by using the white sealing wax and allowing this to be blended into the other colors. In making leaves some of the light yellow wax can be blended into the darker greens to give contrast as well as shading. A little practice will soon teach you how to use these colors on most any design. Sometimes the backgrounds of plaques are shaded and instead of being uneven it is smoothed with a heated knife blade. Start at the top with a light color and blend in darker ones as you go toward the bottom. The colors will blend as the heated knife is applied. It might also be mentioned that all sharp points can quickly be smoothed down by barely touching a heated knife blade to them. As in the background it might be added a good effect can be obtained by "padding" down over the entire surface with a heated knife blade. Many of the necessary materials for Jesso Craft and sealing wax work can be obtained by writing to D. M. Campana Art Co., Chicago, Ill.

This plaque was one cut to order. The shape of the plaque was designed to conform with the decoration. All the Jesso work is in high relief, gold being burnished to make it stand out prominently.

CHAPTER XIV
Recipe for Making Jesso Paste

IF YOU wish to make up your own Jesso paste you can
follow the following recipe. It is advisable, however, to
purchase the already prepared clay in the cans, thereby avoid-
ing any fuss or muss, and you will have more certain success
with a well-tried article. This is what you will need to make
your own Jesso paste:

> 2 lbs. Whiting
>
> ½ pt. LePages Glue
>
> 1 oz. Linseed Oil
>
> 1 oz. Varnish
>
> ½ oz. Powdered Lead White

Sift the lead white and the whiting together so that there
are no lumps. You then take one and one-half cups full of
this mixture and put in a mixing bowl, then pour in slowly
in the following order: One gill of the glue, three teaspoonful
of linseed oil and three teaspoons of varnish. Mix slowly with
a spoon or wooden fork till perfectly smooth. If after carefully
stirring, the mixture seems oily and does not cling to the side
of the bowl, stir longer and add a little glue; and if not of a
consistency that will "pile" up and remain so in a scrolled
effect, add whiting by tablespoonful until proper consistency is
secured. If the mixture is too thick and impossible to stir
thin with a tablespoonful of water. If larger quantities are required it is advisable to mix on a slab with spatula. When not
using, keep Jesso paste in an air tight jar; if it should become dry, moisten with a little water.

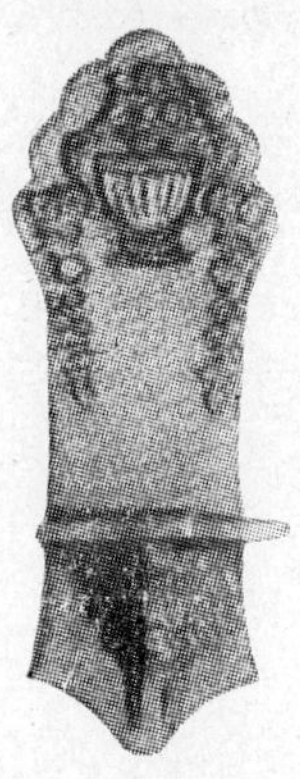

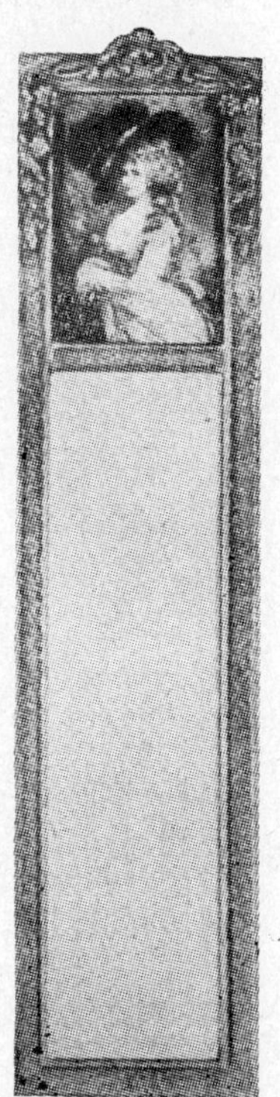

On the wall scone Jesso ornaments have been used and the balance is in fine stipple. The flowers in the ornament have been painted in various colors and the stipple is in gold. The same idea was carried out in the mirror, excepting that the Jesso ornament was placed to extend beyond the top of the frame.

CHAPTER XV
Jewel Decoration

IN THE corners of the plaques and frames colored jewels can be set in the Jesso paste before it has hardened. These are very attractive and an assortment can be obtained at any department store for a small amount. Get these that have a flat back and the size not larger than one-half or five-eighths inch, unless you have a very large piece to make up. We show several pieces in which such jewels have been set.

Flower Pot

Use simple border at top — the one shown is easily copied. Build this up high with Jesso also additional design in center of pot. Pot should be painted in red, center design in red or yellow. Shellac to give a glossy finish. Rim of pot could also be painted in gold bronze, or in fact entire pot in gold and center design in color.

Telephone Screen

The one illustrated is made from three-ply veneer and similar shapes will be found among dealers in art goods, although most of those made are hinged together instead of tied. The entire background was first smooth stippled and then the design of the coat of arms, outlined and then filled in with the raised paste. The same border as used in the plaque is also used at the bottom in the screen. Paint in the design in red, purple or blue and dark green and the background in gold bronze.

Plaque

Purchase a plaque about eight by thirteen and one-half rounded at the top. Set in picture of upright figure in position as shown on plaque. Cover entire balance of surface with clay leaving smooth surface. Draw in your design at top above picture and also draw a margin or border one-half inch wide all around edge of plaque. Build up with Jesso paste then gild and shellac entire plaque includ-ing the picture. Paint the design mo-tifs in emerald green and vermilion. To "antique" dab a mixture of a little raw umber and black oil paint here and there and rub it all over and into the gold with a piece of cheese cloth. Wipe off any excess. Designs for these articles can be obtained in McCall's patterns.

Waste Basket

Usually the waste basket can be purchased already set up and joined together, and then again it can be bought "knock down" and you will have to set it up yourself; sometimes these are made so that the sides are joined together by ribbons.

In the illustration of the waste basket you will notice that the design appears modeled, but as a matter of fact it has been built up with rope and bamboo curbed strips and plain wood strips. The raised design at the top was obtained by nailing down the bamboo strips on the outside and then cover with Jesso paste; at the corners plain straight wood strips were nailed down and lightly covered with clay. The design in center is in relief made with Jesso paste. The border around the design was made with rope, sash cord being used and this then covered with clay. The cord is glued down and a few small nails driven through to make it secure. Balance is covered with clay, giving smooth effect, and it is then colored. A pale green with ornaments in ivory make an attractive basket.

54
ART PUBLICATIONS
All Written and Published by D. M. Campana, Artist
Chicago, Illinois

Popular, Useful and at Moderate Cost
Add 15c Each for Mailing.

———

The Teacher of Oil Paintings. By D. M. Campana.
Teaches the easiest method to learn oil painting. Landscape, figure, animal life, still life. A practical book. (15th Edition.) Price **85c.**

The Teacher of Water Color Painting. By D. M. Campana.
Teaching flowers, figure, landscape, etc., in a plain, clear manner. (12th edition.) Price **85c.**

The Teacher of Landscape Painting. By D. M. Campana.
(Seventh Edition.) Teaches how to start and finish a landscape, how to harmonize effects, colors, etc. Price **85c.**

The Teacher of Drawing. By D. M. Campana.
A book giving a systematic method of learning how to draw from nature. (6th Edition.) Price **$1.00.**

The Teacher of Figure Painting and Portraits. Fourth edition. By D. M. Campana. Teaches how to start and how to finish. Gives colors, methods, etc. Price **85c.**

Books of Monograms and Lettering. By D. M. Campana.
Contains a large variety of all styles (thousands of them). (5th Edition.) Price **85c.**

The Teacher of Pastel Painting. By D. M. Campana.
It teaches how to handle pastel pictures, how to start and how to finish them. Paper to use, quality of pastel, how to fasten them, etc. Price **85c.** (Fifth Edition.)

The Teacher of Geometrical Drawing. By D. M. Campana.
A book of instruction on geometry with very many illustrations and clearly taught. For schools or students. Price **85c.** (2nd Edition.)

The Teacher of Flower and Fruit Painting. By D. M. Campana.
This book explains individual colors to use in painting of flowers and fruit. A practical and useful book. Price **85c.** (Fourth Edition.)

The Teacher of Picture Frame Finishing. By D. M. Campana.
It teaches how to gild, how to burnish, how to apply gold leaf, how to make a frame, etc. Price **85c.** (3rd Edition.)

Art Drawing Made Easy. By D. M. Campana.
A system for beginners to learn the fundamental methods. An easy and practical way to learn drawing. 4th Ed. Price **85c.**

The Teacher of Animal Painting. By D. M. Campana.
It gives the colors to use for varied animals. It teaches the best way to paint them. Many illustrations. Price **85c.** (2nd Ed.)

Stained Glass Decorations Without Baking. By D. M. Campana.
Painted with Crystal Colors, beautiful windows and clear effects, very easily taught by this book. Price **85c.**

The Teacher of Photograph Painting. By D. M. Campana.
Teaches how to tint photographs both for art sake and for commercial purposes. Price **85c.** (3rd enlarged Edition.)

Book, "The Teacher of China Painting." By D. M. Campana.
A very complete text book for beginners and advanced workers. (8th Edition.) Price **85c.**

The Artist and Decorators. By D. M. Campana.
A large collection of high class decorations and artistic suggestions in all styles. A book for ambitious workers, such as decorators, designers, artists, engravers. About 500 ideas. Price **$2.50.**

Greeting Cards For All Occasions. Hundreds of them by D. M. Campana. Price **85c** (new).

Self-Taught Picture Painting. No. 3. By D. M. Campana.
With 10 Pictures in colors. Price **$1.25.** 4th reprint.

Anatomy and Human Form. By D. M. Campana. New. **85c.**

Mirror Making and Painting. By D. M. Campana.
Teaches varied decorations. Price **65c.**

Book—Roses and How to Paint Them. By D. M. Campana.
Teaching method for painting roses in water color, china, oil, silk and other branches. Given exclusively to roses with colored studies. (Fifth Edition.) Price **85c.**

The Teacher of Textile Painting. By D. M. Campana, 3rd Edition.
Teaches how to paint all kinds of cloth, silk, velvet, satin, cotton dresses, hats, tapestry, etc. Price **85c.**

The Teacher of Lamp Shade Making. By D. M. Campana.
Teaches how to build and decorate paper shades, silk shades, cotton shades, etc.—giving all details. Price **85c.**

The Teacher of Jesso Decorating. and Plaque Making.
By D. M. Campana.   (3rd Edition
A booklet guiding you and explaining the best way to start and decorate plaques, book ends, candle sticks, etc. Price **85c.**

The Teacher of Linoleum Printing. By D. M. Campana.
It gives the best method and the correct way to make prints for schools or individuals, with illustrations. Price **65c.**

Enamel Decorations. By D. M. Campana.
On porcelain and glass—with illustrations. Teaches the safest enamels and colors. Describes cause for chipping off, etc. Price **85c.**

The Teacher of Lettering Show Cards and Sign Painting. By D. M.
Campana. **85c.** (Second Edition.)

Amateur Artist Encyclopedia.
Contains over 50 different branches of art and craft. By D. M.
Campana. Price **85c.** 3rd edition.

Book of 1000 Decorations and Ideas. By D. M. Campana.
A variety of conventionalized subjects from nature for all
kinds of decorations. A very popular book. Price **85c.** 2nd Ed.

**The Teacher of Casting, Modeling, Sculpturing, Woodcarving and
Pottery. By D. M. Campana.** Price **85c.** 2nd Edition.
Book of Decorative Designs. No. 1. By D. M. Campana.
Full of pretty borders and ideas for all kinds of decorations.
(Third Edition.) Price **90c.**

Book of Decorative Designs. No. 2. By D. M. Campana.
Contains 191 complete designs of all shapes and styles. (Third
Edition. Price **90c.**

Book on Leather Craft. By D. M. Campana. 3rd Edition.
Explaining tooling, carving, painting, polishing, etc. Illustrated with many patterns for bags, etc. Price **85c.**

Book of Decorative Designs. No. 4.
An entirely different collection of decorative ideas, original
and pretty. Price **90c.**

Historical Ornaments and the Teacher of Designing. By D. M.
Campana. Book No. 5.
A fine collection of Historical Ornaments. Also teaches how
to learn designing. Price **$1.00.**

Interior Decorations. By D. M. Campana. Book No. 6.
Full of pretty suggestions for interior decorations. Price **90c.**

Designs and Patterns for China and Glass Decorations. By D. M.
Campana. Book No. 7. ((3rd Edition.)
A large variety of ideas, good for all kinds of work and craft.
Price **$1.00.**

Book—100 Lustre Color Combinations. By D. M. Campana.
How to make them, with all the latest effects. (Second Edition.) Price **85c.** For china and glass.

Book on Firing Porcelain and Glass. By D. M. Campana.
With directions for stacking, repairing, etc. (Third Edition.)
Price **85c.**

Acid Etchings. By D. M. Campana.
On porcelain and glass—with illustrations. Describes from
beginning to end the whole process of etching in on china and
glass. Price **85c.**

Figurines Made at Home. By D. M. Campana.
Teaches the making and painting. Price **85c.**

Glass Decorations and Firing. By D. M. Campana.
A booklet teaching how to decorate and fire crystal glass. Such method can be followed with any quality of glass. Price **55c.**

Ceramic Photography. By D. M. Campana. 2nd edition.
Gives recipes and methods for making photographs on china and enamels. Price **85c.**

Book of Designs and Color Schemes. By D. M. Campana.
A publication in colors, complete; 120 pages of designs in colors and directions. Better than 6 months' lessons. Price **$10.00.** (For china decorations.)

Studies in Series. (20 Series.) By D. M. Campana.
Each series contains 6 designs in colors with many directions. Flowers, fruit, conventional. Each series **75c.**

Teacher of Batik Painting.
Comprising a variety of textile materials. With full instructions. Price **85c**; mail, **5c.**

Campana's Gold Paint Formula. How to Make It. For Porcelain and Glass. By D. M. Campana.
In paste form to be baked. A valuable secret recipe. **$10.00.**

Art Anatomy and Human Form. By. D. M. Campana.
Finely illustrated. **85c,** mail **10c.**

Teacher of Pottery Made at Home. (New) By D. M. Campana.
Price **85c.**

Teacher of Ceramette Painting. By D. M. Campana.
Steel slab coated with enamel and baked at 2000° F. Painted over with mineral colors and baked at 1500° F. Decorations are everlasting. Something new. Instructions. Price 85c.

Teacher of Commercial Advertising. By D. M. Campana.
A how you do book, in a big field. Price **85c.**
Beginner of China Painting. 35c; mail 5c.

Beginner of Oil Painting. 35c; mail 5c.

Beginner of Water Color Painting. 35c; mail 5c.

NOTICE—The above **54** publications by D. M. Campana are sold at the stores selling artists' materials and art literature.

These books are sold at low prices, contain much useful information on the varied branches of art and are as instructive as any book costing several dollars. If you can't find the wanted book in your store, write the author of this book, D. M. Campana, Artist, Chicago 10, Illinois enclosing the amount specified and you will **receive it** promptly. **Add 15c for mailing.**